# The Night Before Christmas

# The Night Before Christmas

Clement C Moore

Angela Barrett

Sandy Creek

NEW YORK

'Twas the night before Christmas,
when all through the house
Not a creature was stirring,
not even a mouse.

The stockings were hung
by the chimney with care,
In hopes that St. Nicholas
soon would be there.

The children were nestled
all snug in their beds,
While visions of sugarplums
danced in their heads.

And Mamma in her 'kerchief, and I in my cap,
Had just settled down for a long winter's nap,
When out on the lawn there arose such a clatter,

I sprang from the bed to see what was the matter.
Away to the window I flew like a flash,
Tore open the shutters and threw up the sash.

The moon on the breast of the new-fallen snow

Gave a luster of midday to objects below;

When, what to my wondering eyes should appear,

But a miniature sleigh and eight tiny reindeer,

With a little old driver, so lively and quick,

I knew in a moment it must be St. Nick.

More rapid than eagles his coursers they came,

And he whistled, and shouted, and called them by name . . .

"Now, Dasher! Now, Dancer!
Now, Prancer and Vixen!
On, Comet! On, Cupid!
On, Donder and Blitzen!
To the top of the porch!
To the top of the wall!
Now, dash away! Dash away!
Dash away all!"

As dry leaves before
the wild hurricane fly,
When they meet with an obstacle,
mount to the sky;
So up to the house-top
the coursers they flew,
With the sleigh full of toys –
and St. Nicholas, too.

And then, in a twinkling, I heard on the roof
The prancing and pawing of each little hoof.

As I drew in my head and was turning around,
Down the chimney St. Nicholas came with a bound.
He was dressed all in fur, from his head to his foot,
And his clothes were all tarnished with ashes and soot.

A bundle of toys
he had flung on his back,
And he looked like a peddler
just opening his pack.

His eyes, how they twinkled!
His dimples, how merry!
His cheeks were like roses,
his nose like a cherry!

His droll little mouth
was drawn up like a bow,
And the beard on his chin
was as white as the snow!

The stump of a pipe he held tight in his teeth,
And the smoke it encircled his head like a wreath.
He had a broad face and a little round belly
That shook when he laughed, like a bowl full of jelly.

He was chubby and plump — a right jolly old elf,
And I laughed when I saw him, in spite of myself.
A wink of his eye and a twist of his head
Soon gave me to know I had nothing to dread.

He spoke not a word,
but went straight to his work,
And filled all the stockings,
then turned with a jerk . . .

And laying his finger aside of his nose,
And giving a nod, up the chimney he rose.

He sprang to his sleigh, to his team gave a whistle,
And away they all flew like the down of a thistle.
But I heard him exclaim, as he drove out of sight,

## "Merry Christmas to all, and to all a good night!"

For Roger William Barrett, my dear brother – A.B.

**Sandy Creek**
NEW YORK

An Imprint of Sterling Publishing
387 Park Avenue South
New York, NY 10016

SANDY CREEK and the distinctive Sandy Creek logo
are registered trademarks of Barnes & Noble, Inc.

First published in Great Britain in 2012 by Orchard Books, an imprint of Hachette Children's Books.

Illustrations © 2012 by Angela Barrett

This 2012 custom edition is published exclusively for Sandy Creek by Orchard Books.

Design by Tim Rose

ISBN 978-1-4351-4416-3

For information about custom editions, special sales, and premium and corporate purchases,
please contact Sterling Special Sales at 800-805-5489 or specialsales@sterlingpublishing.com.

Manufactured in China

Lot #:
2  4  6  8  10  9  7  5  3  1
08/12

my Birthday · List
1. Dog ♡
2.

For my **good** friend Dan and his sometimes **bad** dogs
—M.B.

Copyright © 2019 by Mike Boldt

All rights reserved. Published in the United States by Doubleday, an imprint of Random House Children's Books,
a division of Penguin Random House LLC, New York.

Doubleday and the colophon are registered trademarks of Penguin Random House LLC.

Visit us on the Web! rhcbooks.com

Educators and librarians, for a variety of teaching tools, visit us at RHTeachersLibrarians.com

*Library of Congress Cataloging-in-Publication Data*
Names: Boldt, Mike, author, illustrator.
Title: Bad dog / by Mike Boldt.
Description: First edition. | New York : Doubleday Books for Young Readers, [2019] |
Summary: A little girl gets a cat as a new pet but insists it's a dog, even if it doesn't act very dog-like.
Identifiers: LCCN 2018024677 (print) | LCCN 2018030242 (ebook) |
ISBN 978-1-9848-4797-3 (hc) | ISBN 978-1-9848-4798-0 (glb) | ISBN 978-1-9848-4799-7 (ebk)
Subjects: | CYAC: Dogs—Fiction. | Cats—Fiction. | Humorous stories.
Classification: LCC PZ7.B635863 (ebook) | LCC PZ7.B635863 Bad 2019 (print) | DDC [E]—dc23

MANUFACTURED IN CHINA
10 9 8 7 6 5 4 3 2 1
First Edition

# BAD DOG

by Mike Boldt

DOUBLEDAY BOOKS FOR YOUNG READERS

Look what I
got for my birthday!

A pet dog!

My dog has black-and-white fur.

Pointy ears.

And a cute little nose.

Her name is Rocky,

and she is a bad dog.

Rocky doesn't listen like good dogs.

"HEY, ROCKY, COME. AWW, COME ON. YOU CAN DO IT, ROCKY! COME HERE, GIRL!"

See?

Rocky is a bad dog.

Good dogs like to
go for walks.

But not Rocky.

And Rocky <u>really</u> doesn't
like other dogs.

She is great
at climbing,
though.

"BAD DOG, ROCKY.
COME DOWN!"

Rocky doesn't listen.
She is a bad dog.

I am teaching Rocky some tricks that good dogs do.

"ROCKY, FETCH!"

"ROCKY, ROLL OVER."

"SHAKE a paw?"

Rocky is not a good dog.

But Rocky
isn't all bad.
Rocky doesn't bark
when the mail
is delivered.

And Rocky
doesn't have

accidents on the floor.

She doesn't chew my toys either—
though she does like to
play with my shoelaces.

What else does Rocky like?

Rocky likes to sleep in the sun.

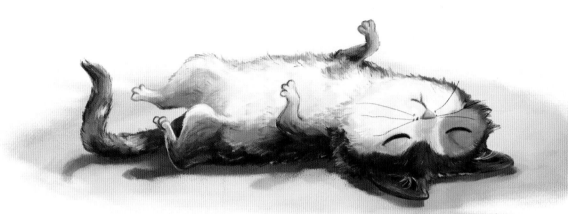

And sleep on Dad's chair.

And sleep on Mom's clothes.

Rocky really likes to sleep.

I thought Rocky liked
to play in the water.

But she is <u>not</u> a fan

of bath time.

"COME DOWN, ROCKY!"

See, Rocky still doesn't listen.

She is a bad dog...

...with black-and-white fur.

Pointy ears.

And a cute little nose.

You know what?

I think Rocky would make

a pretty great cat.

Well, most of the time.

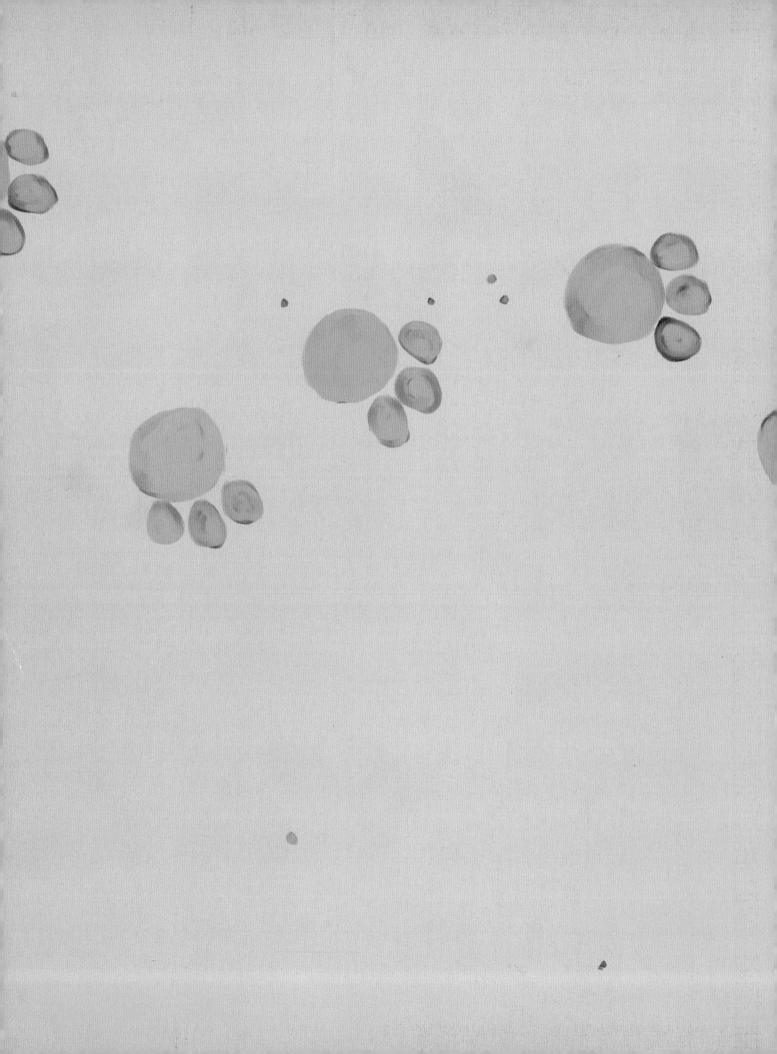